The Health & Happiness Guide
to the Universal Laws

The Health & Happiness Guide to the Universal Laws

WHAT YOU MOST WANT TO KNOW

• • •

Bonnie L. Sax

Copyright © 2016 Bonnie L. Sax

All rights reserved. No part of this book may be reproduced, distributed or transmitted in any form or by any means, including photocopying, recording, or other electronic or mechanical methods, including information storage and retrieval systems, without the prior written permission of the publisher or author, except in the case of brief quotations embodied in critical reviews and certain other noncommercial uses permitted by copyright law. For permission requests, email the author at Bonnie@BonnieSax.com or send your request to 12329 Aviles Circle, Palm Beach Gardens, Florida 33418.

To contact the author or publisher, visit www.BonnieSax.com.

The author of this book does not dispense medical advice or prescribe the use of any technique as a form of treatment for physical, emotional, or medical problems without the advice of a physician, either directly or indirectly. The intent of the author is only to offer information of a general nature to help you in your quest for emotional and spiritual well-being. In the event, you use any of the information in this book for yourself, which is your constitutional right, the author and the publisher assume no responsibility for your actions.

ISBN-13: 9780692806913
ISBN-10: 0692806911

Printed in the United States of America

Table of Contents

Acknowledgements

● ● ●

This book would have never been put to print without some pretty amazing people. Given my subject matter, I know that every one of them was put in my life for a bigger purpose than just nudging me along as an author.

To David, Sarah, and Matthew, you have been an endless source of support and examples of the Universal Laws in action. Your love and willingness to help me mean so much. To Susan, you gave me my first spiritual nudge, and then so many more along the way. You are proof of the people placed in your life to move you along. To Greg, Melissa, Karen, Pat, and Holly, you are part of my healing team and some of the most amazing teachers on the planet. To Lily, you are beyond a business partner and fellow adventurer. You have encouraged me to push the boundaries and dream bigger. To Kat, thank you for reminding me finish my thoughts. To every one of my friends that started out as Akashic Records students, thank you for your unwavering support and confidence in what we doing together. To everyone that has picked up this book to discover more about who they are, thank you.

• • •

IINSPIRED BY THE INSTITUTE FOR INTEGRATIVE NUTRITION

Prior to learning to read the Akashic Records, I decided to become a health coach through the Institute for Integrative Nutrition. Over the years I had considered becoming a life coach but the timing was never quite right. When a respected friend became a health coach, I decided to become one, too.

As it turns out, the coaching element has been an integral part of my reading of the Akashic Records, and my training in holistic wellness and health coaching laid the foundation for writing this book.

IIN offers a truly comprehensive Health Coach Training program that invites students to deeply explore the things that are most nourishing to them. From the physical aspects of nutrition and eating wholesome foods that work best for each individual person, to the concept of Primary Food – the idea that everything in life including our spirituality, career, relationships, and fitness contribute to our inner and outer health – IIN helped me reach optimal health and balance. This inner journey unleashed the passion that compelled me to share what I've learned and inspire others.

Beyond personal health, IIN offers training in health coaching, as well as business and marketing training. Students who choose to pursue this field, complete the program equipped with the communication skills and branding knowledge they need to create a fulfilling career encouraging and supporting others to reach their own health goals.

From renowned wellness experts as Visiting Teachers to the convenience of their online learning platform, this school has changed my life and I believe it will do the same for you. I invite you to learn more about the Institute for Integrative Nutrition and explore how the Health Coach Training Program can help you transform your life. Feel free to contact me to hear more about my personal experience at www.BonnieSax.com or call (844) 315-8456 to learn more.

Introduction

$\bullet \quad \bullet \quad \bullet$

I ADMIT THAT I DIDN'T understand the Law of Attraction or The Secret when everyone was buzzing about it. I understood that like attracts like because I could see it happening in my own life. I attracted friends that liked to do similar activities on the weekends, our children participated in similar activities, and we volunteered at similar places.

What I didn't understand about the Law of Attraction was how to apply that information in my own life to attract the things I thought I wanted. Of course, I wanted more money. I thought more money meant more vacations, more stuff for my kids, and less worries. I wanted good health and happiness for my family but I didn't know how to attract it.

I didn't understand what I needed to say, hang on my refrigerator, or write on my bathroom mirror. Did I need to cut out more pictures? Whatever it was, I wasn't doing it. I was getting some of what I wanted but I wasn't getting it all.

That changed at the beginning of 2016. I still wasn't sure how the Law of Attraction worked, but when a copy of *Ask and It Is Given: Learning to Manifest Your Desires* fell off my book shelf, I sat down and started reading. The book was written by Esther and Jerry Hicks about the Law of Attraction and in it Esther speaks for the collective consciousness called Abraham.

A few minutes into the first chapter and I was entranced. I understood the concepts and I wanted more information. I ordered Abraham Hicks' *The Law of Attraction* book on tape, and *Getting into the Vortex: Guided Meditations*

CD and User's Guide. I googled the Law of Attraction and discovered there were over 100 other Universal Laws.

The more I read about the Universal Laws, the more I was intrigued. Most of them made sense so I started talking about them and working with them in my own life. It wasn't long before I noticed that decisions were easier to make, more opportunities were available to me, and I struggled less in creating what I wanted. This was good information, and I wanted to share what I discovered with others.

Within a week of this realization, two books were put in my office by mistake with clear references to the Universal Laws. One friend suggested I read about the Law of Compensation. Another friend stopped me in the grocery store to ask me when I was writing my book.

Write a book? That was a strange question to ask me in the grocery store.

Then I remembered the book that I said I wanted to write in a goal-setting class I attended when I was 25. I didn't have a title or subject matter but I knew I would write a book one day.

During my research, I discovered that not much had been written about the Universal Laws. I found a few books and a dozen websites but that was it. It seemed unusual considering how much has been written about the Law of Attraction.

Suddenly my path became clear. The book I would write was about the Universal Laws. It was going to be a health and happiness guide because that is what people long for. I now pass it on to you with the hope that you enjoy this voyage of discovery as much as I have, and I wish you all the best.

● ● ●

MY EXPERIENCE WITH THE AKASHIC RECORDS

More than two years ago, a dear friend gave me the gift of an Akashic Records reading. I didn't know what was involved in a reading, and I wasn't too sure how to describe the Akashic Records but I knew they had something to do with past lives, and that I could ask questions I had about the next phase of my life.

At the time of the reading, I was studying to become a health coach and I wondered how I was going to help people. My question was: Would I coach people individually, teach classes about eating well, or work in a doctor's office? I didn't get the answer that I thought I would from the Akashic Records. Instead of cluing me in about my health coach practice, the practitioner that was reading my records said, "You are going to read the Akashic Records."

Huh? That didn't make sense although it piqued my interest. I rephrased the question asking how I would use my health coach certification.

"You will use your coaching skills in reading the Akashic Records."

After 25 minutes of getting the same kind of answer to almost every question, I asked the practitioner, "What do I need to do next?"

She suggested I read the book, "How to Read the Akashic Records" by Linda Howe. By chapter 4, I understood that reading the Akashic Records was exactly what I had been looking for to fulfill the next phase of my life.

I became a certified Akashic Records teacher and healing practitioner. While I read my own Records and I read the Records for others, my passion is to teach people to read their own Records.

The word Akasha is Sanskrit for "primary substance" or "that out of which everything is made." The Akasha is so sensitive that the slightest vibration is felt and recorded. These recordings are stored in the Akashic Records and includes everything that has ever been thought, said, or done in the Universe since your soul's inception. This information is available to you by accessing a dimension of consciousness where you are both conscious and Divinely connected at the same time.

Think of a meditative state in which your eyes are open, and you can speak, write, and interact with those around you.

A particularly cool aspect of the Akashic Records is that you can ask your spiritual guides almost anything you want to know about. This includes your life purpose, past life lessons, and insights into every issue in your life. One of my favorite things to do in the Records is to heal the old stories that no longer work for me, and to realign with my soul's purpose.

When I read the Akashic Records, I am engaging in a conversation with spiritual guides called Masters, Teachers, and Loved Ones. I ask a question, and thoughts and concepts come into my mind much in the same way that you talk to yourself every day. With intention and practice, I translate those conversations into words that can be understood.

One day I opened my Records and asked my guides what was next for me to do. The answer was that it was time to write the book, and that I was to use the wisdom of the Akashic Records as a resource.

So, I sat down to write. Each time I wrote I was accessing two types of information. The first came from my own research, personal experiences, and tapping into my higher consciousness or inner knowing.

The second source came from my Records in the form of direct messages from my Masters, Teachers, and Loved Ones who are the keepers of the Akashic Records. These direct messages are featured in italic text throughout this book.

Below is the first direct message that I received. I wanted to know why I didn't understand the Law of Attraction before, but now it seemed to make so much sense. Here is the answer I received:

So much has been written about the Law of Attraction and you're correct that it has seemed like a very confusing law. Part of that is context. You saw the Law as a single Law instead of seeing all the Universal Laws together. If we gave you just a picture of Van Gogh's eye, you would think it was a strange picture for sure. But when we expand your view and show you the entire portrait, it makes more sense.

The same is true with the Law of Attraction.

Like attracts like. Always. And we are talking completely from an energy perspective. A dog can attract a cat as its best friend because it needs what the cat offers from an energy perspective. People who don't understand the Law might think dogs and cats are different. Yes, we agree, but look deeper.

They both need to learn that even though they are different species, they both need friendship and companionship. That's the energy that brought them together. We always attract what we need energetically.

The whole idea of life is to experience what you need to experience. You've already experienced perfection, bliss and what it is like to know completeness. Believe it or not, you already know God, totally and completely. You've come to earth to experience being human.

As a human, you've experienced many lifetimes and you can see these lifetimes as so many books in a book series.

For example, Book 1 is the story of you as an ancient tribesman seeing what you are capable of in a primitive society. In Book 2, you were a woman during the time when Mother Earth was revered, and women were respected for their wisdom and connection to Mother Earth. In Book 3, you only lived to the age of seven because of a mysterious disease. And so on.

Each book or lifetime has had different subplots and characters. Your family, friends and people you met changed with each book, but those you interacted with were also living out their own lives in their own books.

Every book has had its own details, experiences, and memories both good and bad. For the most part, the stories repeated themselves over lifetimes. Life was hard and unless you lived a life of power and privilege, you felt like you were never getting ahead. The rules kept everyone in their place.

Now, the rules have changed. You have access to the Universal Laws and they apply to everyone equally.

We want you to know the Universal Laws. We want you to know how powerful you are. We want you to once again remember the secrets of the Universe. It is your Divine right. Come let's remember them together.

Note to the Reader

As you read about the Universal Laws, there may be times when the description makes perfect sense and other times when you find yourself reading it over and over again, struggling with the concept. There were quite a few times when this happened to me. The reason is because we are human, and our egos, personalities, and individual perspectives sometimes stand in the way of our understanding.

For those of you who are meticulous with details and want to know everything all at once, you might be frustrated. If this disturbs you, please skip to the Law of Reflection to read about how to release some of your concerns.

For those of you who are not detail-oriented but are worried you should be, relax and understand that the details really do not matter. Start at the beginning and read through to the end. If you find yourself still confused or disturbed that you aren't, please see the Law of Reflection to understand why this happens.

For those of you who would like more information on the Universal Laws or the Akashic Records, please check the References section.

For everyone reading this, please understand that the more you bring an attitude of play to exploring the Universal Laws, the more the fun will show up for you. This is not life and death information to understand. There is no life and death here. There's only on and on and on.

● ● ●

The Universe supports the reality of your beliefs absolutely.
When you believe you must struggle for abundance,
Then it will bring about situations that are conducive to struggle;
When you believe you cannot experience love without pain,
The Universe will give you exactly that – love with pain;
When you believe it takes time for an
illness to heal – then so it will.
There is not a single force opposing you, there is
only ONE force supporting you absolutely.
It is called LOVE, the force that birthed you,
that created you in its own image.
This love is so magnanimous it will give you exactly and
absolutely whatever it is that your reality entails.
Change your beliefs and you change your reality.

Author Unknown

● ● ●

CHAPTER 1

What are the Universal Laws?

● ● ●

THE UNIVERSAL LAWS ARE THE governing laws that keep everything in the Universe moving in perfect harmony. Once you understand and apply them to your daily life, you will experience a transformational shift in your thinking.

Are you ready to get started? Here is a message about the Universal Laws:

Let's imagine that we are playing a game. We grabbed the game from the closet, set up the board on the table, placed all the game pieces and pulled out the rules. Those rules are the Universal Laws. The rules give structure to the game, and everyone has agreed to follow them. A game with no rules is an experience without intention. Unlike the games played on your planet, no one breaks these rules. Every being respects and adheres to the Universal Laws.

We understand that this is a hard concept for many of you to take in. First, you are coming to the awareness that there is a Universe, something bigger and beyond your planet. Second, there is a knowing that if there are rules to follow there must be beings that exist to follow those rules. Lastly, there is the disbelief that no one breaks the rules. Your belief is that everyone breaks the rules.

To make understanding the Laws easier, please be comfortable in naming them what works for you. Some of you would rather call them God's Laws or The Unbreakable Laws. Play with the words until you are comfortable. We call them the Universal Laws but we satisfied with whatever words work best for you.

The first Law is that we all come from the same Source, the same energy. This Law reminds you that we are smaller parts of the whole. The next Law reminds you that you created your life for the experiences you want to have.

And so on. Every rule or Law was put into place to help. No Law was created to restrict or hinder the players. This is important to remember. You may feel screwed by the Law of Reflection but that is your perspective to re-examine as you become aware.

Remember, everything is there for your increased awareness and learning. When you understand that what you are feeling is a clue to what you want to experience, you can relax into the process and find more joy.

It's always about joy. Keep finding the joy.

CHAPTER 2

The Law of One

● ● ●

Everything is connected. We are all one.

Every soul, both living and in spirit, is plugged in to the universal consciousness. You are plugged into the great energy called God, and so is every other being. Just like all parts of you are part of God so, too, is every other being. Nothing is left out. Everything that has ever been said, done or thought is a part of God. As you say, the good, the bad and the ugly. Your angelic parts, evil parts and the parts you hide from everyone else. That is the Law of One we want you to know.

AS A CHILD, I WAS fascinated by the idea that we are all so much alike physically. Two arms, two legs, two eyes, one nose, one mouth, two hands, four fingers and a thumb on each hand. One heart, two lungs, one digestive system, one reproductive system, and skin covering all of it. Yes, the skin has different shades, more hair, or more wrinkles but everyone still has it. Even the people I knew that did not have all their appendages still had a place where they used to be.

As an adult, I am fascinated with the similarity of our human experiences. Friends I make around the world struggle with the same issues that my friends and I deal with here – dating, jobs, children, family, personally relating in the world and so much more. It does not matter what religion we are, our sexual orientation, or our country of origin. When we strip those details away, we are the same and are experiencing the same kind of human stories.

Throw a dart at a map of the world and in that place, there are people dealing with heartbreak, falling in love, giving birth or reconciling with the death of a loved one, feeling alone, feeling judged, or feeling worried about something. Everyone everywhere is busy experiencing life.

This is the Law of One in action. Even though we may look very different we are the same. We are a part of God; like individual snowflakes on the snow-covered peaks of Mount Everest.

Did you know that every one of the cells in your body is a being that is completely able to move, breathe, grow, take in and excrete nutrients, feel and reproduce, all with a desire to have a personal connection to Source [God, Creator or the collective consciousness]? Within each cell, every neutron, electron and proton is capable of the same activities. These protons, electrons and neutrons are part of the cell, which is part of an organ, which is part of a body, which is part of God. We are smaller pieces of the much larger picture.

Once you understand that everyone on the planet is connected to the same Source, it is much easier to extend awareness, understanding, and even forgiveness to your fellow human beings.

When you see that we are more alike than different and that my story is your story, you can begin to trust your neighbor, love your fellow countryman, and make peace with the people on the other side of the planet.

Have you seen the commercial where a man walking down the street notices water dripping off a roof onto a woman selling fruits and vegetables? He helps her move her tables, and he pushes a dried-up pot of flowers over to the drip. The woman thanks him with an apple that he gives to a man farther down the street begging for food. The beggar thanks him and walks away to help an elderly woman across the street. The elderly woman sits down on a bench to soothe a crying child and calm the distraught mother. Once the child is quiet, the elderly woman moves on. The pot of flowers next to the woman selling fruits and vegetables starts to perk up and bloom with the extra water.

With one man's desire to help a woman be more comfortable, six people are positively affected—perhaps more. Whether you realize it or not, our lives are intertwined and we are all connected.

● ● ●

Putting the Law of One into Practice

Living the Universal Law of One means that you are constantly looking for ways to build bridges and to connect with every other living being on earth. This includes animals, plants, rocks, minerals, and everything of the earth. We are all here to experience life and evolve, and the following suggestions for living the Universal Law of One can help:

- Allow 15 minutes to meditate on gratitude. Simply settle into your seat with your feet on the floor and your hands in your lap. Begin thinking of people who you are grateful for in your life. There is no particular order or way to do this. The only rule is to continue for the full 15 minutes. Notice that after a while you may find yourself mentally thanking the man who stocked the shelves at the grocery store, or the person who delivered your favorite book to your door. Keep going. Recognize how we are all connected on a very real level.
- Buy a children's watercolor set and with some watercolor paper and a cup of water in front of you, begin painting whatever suits you. As you dip your brush into the water and then into the paint, consider that God is the water that brings the color to life. Each one of us on the planet is a paint color. We are all the same paint, but are just slightly different. Frame your picture when you are finished.
- Begin to pay attention to the words that are spoken around you. Notice the language that brings people together and compare it to the words that separate people. Consider adding more words that unite us, remind us that we are all the same regardless of what we see on the outside.

*   Consider all the things that have changed since you were born. Streets, buildings, and people who have come and gone during your life in various ways, opinions that you have had and changed. Become aware that even as things change, many things stay the same. Notice what has changed and what has stayed the same.

*   When an animal or insect invades your space, consider removing it with love and respect. Capture a bug or lizard and release it back outside. Remember that we are all connected, even the insects and bugs.

*   If you have the opportunity to give advice to a friend or loved one, take a moment to see how the Law of One applies. That is, think about how your advice will affect everyone surrounding the situation. If your friend wants guidance on how to relate to a coworker, consider how your advice will affect the coworker, the other employees, your friend's family, and the coworker's family. Will everyone be positively affected by your advice, or negatively influenced? Always be an advocate for bringing people together and making them feel better about themselves.

CHAPTER 3

The Law of Reincarnation & Karma and The Law of Magnetic Affinities

● ● ●

You chose your life for the lessons you wanted to experience. You chose your birth place, date, time, circumstances, parents, astrological sign, character, personality, abilities, and plan for your life. Each life requires a different set of circumstances, personality, traits, and people. With each life experience, you are in service to the universal consciousness. You are living your expressed purpose.

LONG BEFORE I STARTED EXPLORING this metaphysical path, I believed in reincarnation. It made sense to me that the life I was currently living could not be all there was. Why would we come here to live and die with no purpose other than what we accomplished in one life?

Reincarnation, or the idea that your soul comes back in another body for another lifetime, gives more purpose to this life. You reincarnate to continue the work or heal the situation that you left unfinished in a previous life.

Reincarnation explains why certain talents and abilities come naturally to some people and not to others, like the three-year-old who plays an entire concerto after his third time plunking on the piano. He was a skilled pianist or composer in another life, and brought that knowledge with him into this one.

Reincarnation explains the déjà vu feeling you have when you meet someone for the first time and feel like you've met before. Have you ever visited a new place that somehow felt familiar, or done something for the first time that felt completely comfortable? That instant recognition you noticed is your soul's acknowledgement of your previous life experience.

The Law of Reincarnation and Karma states that until you have resolved your karma—the deeds that you must do to restore balance and harmony due to your actions in past lives—you will continue to reincarnate. You decide before incarnation what you most need to learn and experience, and you arrange these lessons with other souls who have shared histories and match your karmic needs. These souls are with you on earth.

These arrangements are made during your time in between lives, in that space where you rest before you step into another life. This is a place where you examine everything that happened in the previous lifetime to discover and clarify what you experienced and learned. You review your choices – good, bad, and indifferent – and then catalog what your next steps might be to make progress on your soul's journey back to God.

Rest assured that you do not make these decisions by yourself. My guides described this process as each soul sitting in a conference room around a large table with Masters, Teachers, Loved Ones, and other guides providing input for the next life. Guides are coming and going, pulling information from various past lives and discussing various scenarios. You might see it in a different way because we are each shown the references that make the most sense from our individual perspective. I have a business background so my reference is a conference room.

It is important to remember that we plan every detail of our next life. This is the Law of Magnetic Affinities in action. You choose your parents for what you will experience growing up – a strict household, one with very little structure, or something in between. In this lifetime, you might have a parent that struggles with addiction, perfectionism or abuse so that you can clear that karma. You have a dozen siblings so you can learn to work with a lot of different types of people, or you are an only child to appreciate being by yourself. Everything is designed for the experience you want to have.

You choose your birth time, place, and arrangement of the stars and planets. Your astrological chart dictates much of your personality, characteristics, traits, and relationships which will play out in your life. Different stories require different personalities. If you are going to play the part of a mad scientist you will have a different astrological chart than if you are going to be the quiet librarian.

You can look at your personality as comprising the collective experiences that you have stored in your memory over lifetimes. You are used to thinking of your personality as it relates to just this life. In actuality, many of the qualities you like and dislike have followed you through lifetimes. You are working to clean out what hasn't worked, and strengthen what does work.

You make contracts and agreements with other souls to have certain experiences, to learn aspects of being human, and to support other souls to do the same. These sacred contracts help you understand why certain people appear in your life at just the right time with just the right information for what you need to continue on to the next part of your journey.

The essential idea of these two Universal Laws is that when you understand that you have arranged your life exactly as it is unfolding; you will have a deeper patience and awareness about why things are happening. It is easier to release the anxiety, worry, stress, and the need to control events that happens when you believe that the events in your life are random and without purpose.

● ● ●

Putting the Law of Magnetic Affinities into Practice

- ❀ Seek out an astrological reading from a professional. Discover the insights into your life that are available in your chart. Take one piece of new information and look for ways that it shows up or does not show up in your life. How is it accurate—or not?
- ❀ Consider your own life and the choices that you have made to get you to where you are now. Take one scenario – a career path or a relationship – and play out all the options that were available to you at the time you made the decision. Consider the consequences of making a different decision. Would you have ended up in the same

place or somewhere different? How was your choice the best option at the time?

❋ Make a list of five qualities you love about yourself, and five qualities you wish you could change. Consider how each of them makes up who you are as an individual. Be mindful about when you feel yourself being pulled into a judgmental viewpoint. How have each of these qualities, both those you like and those you don't, played their part in getting you to where you are today?

CHAPTER 4

The Law of Divine Timing

● ● ●

Everything happens exactly as it is supposed to happen. You are exactly where you planned to be for your experience.

FROM A YOUNG AGE, MY children learned what I firmly believe – that everything happens for a reason, and part of our work in the world is to make that reason be worthwhile. Understanding that everything happens exactly as it is supposed to happen is the Law of Divine Timing.

At every moment, your energy is being translated into thoughts, words, emotions and actions to create all your experiences. This provides you with the opportunity to resolve your Karma and align with your purpose.

This is easiest to believe when everything is going in your favor: Of course I was supposed to pass that class with an A, get that perfect job, or find the ideal place to live.

It's much more difficult to accept this law when it feels like things are conspiring against you: Why isn't anyone calling you back for a job interview? Why on earth would your brother commit suicide? Why is everyone against you? When things aren't going the way you want, it is much harder to accept Divine Timing.

I understand. Crappy things happen in everyone's life, including mine.

This is the exact time to remember the Law of Magnetic Affinities, and the idea that this was organized to happen exactly as it has. This is the time to ask why this event happened at this time.

For example, why does murder exist? Assuming you accept that everything happens as it is supposed to, that would include both the murdered and murderer making an agreement prior to incarnation. What lessons can be learned from this agreement?

Certainly, there are personal lessons for the murderer including personal responsibility and a realization that their actions have ramifications. Whether they realize it or not is another kind of discussion.

There are karmic lessons for the person who is murdered, and there are opportunities for understanding and forgiveness for the people affected by the murder. These opportunities can be life-altering.

In some cases, the murder results in a change of society's perspective, beliefs, laws or ways of doing things. It was the murder of Amber Rene Hagerman, a nine-year-old girl from Texas who was abducted and murdered in 1996, that led to the creation of the AMBER alert system. AMBER alerts, part of the Federal Broadcast System, have since saved over 9,000 children's lives since their implementation in the late 1990s. Her death was given meaning.

Perhaps it is a murder that causes people to start a movement to reduce gun violence; but perhaps it doesn't take just one. If the society isn't paying attention or has conflicting values, perhaps it takes 10, 100, or even 1,000 deaths.

Maybe it's just one death that wakes someone up to making different life choices. After taking six bullets from a rival gang member and watching his friend die, Jose Vasquez became the outreach coordinator for a Milwaukee civic organization. The former gang member now helps youth-at-risk avoid making his same mistakes. He has saved lives and set hundreds of young people on a different path.

The difficulty in understanding the Law of Divine Timing is the element of trust that everything happens for a reason, and that you will understand it in Divine Timing.

Did you grow up in a household that taught Divine Timing? Did you learn a respect for events unfolding exactly as they are planned? I didn't, and it is sometimes a struggle to be patient enough to let the process happen naturally.

It is a learned behavior to trust that there is a silver lining to every story. Once you believe that there is a big picture unfolding in ways that aren't understandable to you yet, it is easier to accept each event in your life for exactly what it is — an experience, one that you asked for and received whether you were aware of the asking.

●　●　●

Putting the Law of Divine Timing into Practice

*   Consider something positive that happened in your life. Take the time to examine what happened so you can define it as a positive experience. How did you grow and develop, and what did you learn? Look for the appreciation of the experience.
*   Consider something negative that happened in your life. Take some time to examine what happened so you can define it as a negative experience. Find an appreciation for the growth and awareness that you have acquired.
*   Train your brain to search for the positive perspective in everything that happens in your life for two weeks. You don't have to believe the positive point of view to practice seeing it. You are simply shifting your thinking, and belief will come with more practice.

CHAPTER 5

The Law of Vibration and Energy

● ● ●

Everything in the Universe has a vibration. That vibration is created by the rapid movement of the smallest piece of matter—energy. Everything starts here.

ONE OF THE CONSEQUENCES OF Einstein's theory of special relativity was the mathematical equation $E=mc^2$. It means that energy and mass are equivalent and transmutable, or that all matter is made up of energy. It was a transformative thought in 1905 when it was published. Now quantum physicists have shown that although matter appears to be solid to you and me, when looked at through a high-powered microscope its smallest components (molecules, atoms, neutrons, electrons and quanta) are mostly empty space interspersed with energy. It is understood that the difference between types of matter is the frequency of the vibration that makes it up.

You are energy. I am energy. Everything on the planet is energy.

The Law of Vibration and Energy states that anything that exists in our Universe, whether seen or unseen, is in its simplest form pure energy. This energy is constantly moving and exists as a vibration, frequency or pattern. All matter, thoughts and feelings have their own different vibrational frequency.

An orange vibrates at a different frequency than a candy bar. More specifically, the orange vibrates at a higher, lighter frequency than the candy bar. An organic orange vibrates at a higher and lighter frequency than a conventional orange. This is true of all organic food. Isn't it interesting that healthier foods vibrate at a higher and lighter frequency?

There are no coincidences. Higher and lighter vibrations are healthier for the body. Lower and denser frequencies create more dis-ease and dis-comfort.

The idea of different frequencies extends to people, too. Your best friend has a frequency that resonates with you. They say "birds of a feather flock together." You hang out with people you like and relate to, and who relate to you. You socialize with people vibrating at a similar frequency.

Have you ever had a friendship end after one of you changed your common interest or hobby? Perhaps one of you moved away or left the job you had in common. After a while you saw less of each other, and then communicated only through common friends. From an energy perspective, the two of you started vibrating at different frequencies, and the friendship was difficult to maintain.

There is also a vibration scale for moods. At the high end of frequency is complete joy, and at the low end is complete misery. In between are all the different moods and emotions available to us.

Fear vibrates at a slow and heavy frequency along with anger, frustration and depression. These emotions are like the piano keys far to the left where the sounds are deeper and the tones are lower. They are the bass sounds, dark and energetically slow. In contrast, love, harmony and calm vibrate at faster and lighter frequencies. They are like the piano keys to the right where the sounds are higher pitched and the tones are sharper.

Where each of us fall on the scale varies on a daily basis—sometimes by the hour. There are times when we are feeling dark, moody, frightened or worried. At these times, we are more to the left in the piano keyboard analogy. When we are satisfied, content, feeling silly or having fun, we are more to the right.

The magic of this vibrational scale is that you can shift your mood at any time, simply by choosing a thought that is a little higher than where you currently are. If I'm disappointed about not going on a date Friday night, I can improve my mood with another thought: I'll go out on Saturday night instead. I have friends to go out with on Friday night. Any positive thought will work. Several positive thoughts in a row and you'll find yourself leaping up the vibrational scale.

The opposite is true as well. If you're looking to lower your vibration, a more negative thought will get you there. Worry, fret, concern, and anger will move you quickly down the scale.

Intuitively you will want to be around people who have a similar or higher vibration than you. It is most comfortable for your body to be in harmony. Someone who vibrates significantly lower or higher will cause the body to be inharmonious. You might realize that as your vibration changes, so do some of your relationships, your career, and your health.

If you are looking to raise your vibration, you will want to find ways to do it over time. Find music, books, and people that make you happy. Eat healthier by choosing foods that are organic, good for your body and will energize you. Do work that is satisfying and take on a new hobby. Add more movement to your life with activities that naturally raise your vibration like exercise, yoga, tai chi, nature hikes, or a water sport.

The idea of different frequencies and densities applies to your thoughts as well. Actually, it begins with your thoughts! As your conscious mind thinks habitually about thoughts of a certain quality and density, these thoughts become imbedded within your subconscious mind. Think about them often enough and they become the dominant vibration which sets up an attraction to other similar vibrations in your life.

The average human has 60,000 – 80,000 thoughts a day with up to 80% of them being unconscious or out of your awareness. According to the Law of Vibration every thought, action, and word is also energy and sets up a frequency or pattern. You might not intend to put yourself down consciously, but how many times do you look in the mirror unconsciously and notice the blemish about yourself before the beauty? What percentage of your thoughts are conscious and positive?

Take another look at the definition of $E=mc^2$. Energy and mass are equivalent and transmutable. Transmutable means that energy changes form. Consider a city building that has been abandoned. At first it appears that it does not change at all from day to day, or week to week. Come back a year or two later, and there are chips in the paint and missing tiles on the steps. Another few years later and there are shifts in the foundation, broken windows and the doors are off their hinges. The energy of the building is changing form.

What happens to the city building can happen to you, too. You are energy and capable of changing form in the same way. If you abandon yourself, stop growing and improving, you will notice breakdowns in your physical form. Stop exercising or eating well and notice your body's response. Cease feeding your soul and expanding your awareness and notice your heart's response.

● ● ●

How the Law of Vibration and Energy Shows Up in Your Life

Once you become aware that everything has a vibration or a frequency, you begin to understand that everything that comes into your awareness is vibrating at a level like yours, higher than yours or lower than yours. When it's similar, you just feel good, or you might call this normal. You are probably not even taking vibration into account. You simply move through your day, checking things off your list and enjoying your life.

You are continually drawn to things that vibrate at your level or above. You have friends that you absolutely love to be around. They are self-confident, fun, happy, gracious and they have integrity and a clear sense of purpose. You can think of other positive descriptions for these friends. They vibrate at a higher frequency and if you are reading this book, you want to be around those.

What about the times when you notice something is vibrating at a lower level than you? This shows up as something that makes you feel irritable, annoyed or just generally not good. If it's something simple like something someone said or did it's often easy to dismiss it, let it blow over, and then you go back to vibrating at your higher level.

When it begins to happen on a more regular basis, or is due to a recurring pattern at work or a relationship that no longer suits you, the irritation turns into something bigger. Perhaps it shows up as frustration, anger, or a desire to get out of the situation. Longer exposure to the out-of-sync vibe will show up as symptoms in your body or your mind.

For example, working at a job that you hate could create high blood pressure, which would turn into heart disease and result in a heart attack. The first symptom is your body trying to tell you that something is out of sync. When you don't listen, the issue and repercussions escalate.

The analogy I get in the Records is a well-tuned guitar that plays beautiful music, and one of the strings goes slightly out of tune. It's vibrating at the wrong frequency to be harmonious. The beautiful music turns into something that is a little off to even the untrained ear. When it gets a little more out of tune, the song might be unrecognizable. If the string breaks, the music ends.

● ● ●

You as a Vibration

Everything about you is a vibration. You chose the details of your life for the particular energy it held and what it would manifest in your life. You chose your name and telepathically imparted it to your parents before you were incarnated because of the vibration it holds.

If you google the phrase Name Numerology you can find out the energy and vibration of your name. When it is spoken, your name calls in your life lessons and life purpose.

In numerology, each letter in the alphabet corresponds to a number. A is 1, B is 2, C is 3, D is 4, E is 5, F is 6, G is 7, H is 8 and I is 9. Then the numbers go back to 1 so J is 1 and K is 2 and so on. Calculate your first name's vibration number by using this system. My name is BONNIE so it is $2 + 6 + 5 + 5 + 9 + 5$. Add the numbers together and then add those two digits together to get one number. For BONNIE, the numbers add up to 32, and when you add those two numbers together, $3+2=5$. That is my first name vibration number.

After calculating your first name vibration number, you can look up its numerological meaning. People with a 5 are energetic, freedom-loving, versatile, social and quick thinking on the positive side, and chaotic, self-indulgent and careless on the negative side. This is a simplistic overview. A session with a numerologist would give you more detail and understanding.

The same is true of your birthdate, birth location, and time of birth. This information is used to create your astrological chart. If you have not had your chart done, it is an interesting perspective into another aspect of who you are. It is amazing how much a numerologist or astrologer knows about you by looking at your name, birthdate, birth time, and birth location.

● ● ●

PUTTING THE LAW OF VIBRATION AND ENERGY INTO PRACTICE

- Consider having a numerology forecast, an Akashic Records reading, a tarot card reading, or an astrological chart done for another perspective on who you are energetically. There are resources listed in the back of this book.
- When you notice that you are feeling a lower density or vibration, think a positive thought. Find something to be grateful for and focus on detailing that, or create another grateful experience. Practice this for one minute and then notice your vibration. Did your vibration change?
- Realign your thoughts by watching YouTube videos on vibrational frequencies for healing. Play one and see if you notice a difference in your thoughts and feelings after 20 minutes.
- Investigate the scientific work of Dr. Masaru Emoto, who studied the effect of words and their different frequencies on water. Consider singing the words LOVE, ABUNDANCE, JOY or whatever seems

most appropriate for you into a glass of water that you drink every day. Do you notice a difference in your vibration?

❧ Begin noticing the energy around you at different times of the day. Determine whether it is an energy you want to be around. Becoming conscious of your surroundings helps you create sustained good feelings and a higher vibration.

CHAPTER 6

The Law of Manifestation

● ● ●

You are manifesting all the time. You are constantly creating the world around you by your thoughts, ideas, and beliefs. You are the creator of your life. This is a powerful statement when you truly step into your understanding of your abilities. You have created all of this, all that you see—every rock, animal and mineral, every bit of technology, stick of furniture and everything in between. You are powerful creators.

IN THE SPIRITUAL COMMUNITY, MANIFESTING is a buzzword. Every other person is talking about what they are manifesting and how they are doing it. The truth is that every one of us is spiritual and we are creating all the time. We may not like what we are manifesting but changing that is a matter of understanding the process.

Everything starts with a thought or an idea, which is followed by an action. Put enough actions together and you've created an experience. Put enough of the same type of experiences together and you've created a belief. Once you have a belief in place, you have created your reality. Continue putting thoughts, actions, experiences and beliefs together, and all you've manifested a life.

Take your lucky socks, for example. You wore your purple socks with yellow polka dots to the first game of the season, and your team won. You wore them for the next game by chance, they won again, and you start to think it's your purple socks. You wear them to every game and your team has a perfect season. More than likely, you believe at least a little that your purple socks played a part in the team's winning streak. Perhaps you just aren't willing to take a chance that it isn't the socks. Whether it's true or not, you've created a reality that says lucky purple socks mean a winning season.

This is the Universal Law of Manifestation. The power of the Law comes not in knowing how to create your life, because that will happen without you putting much thought into it. The power is in understanding that your thoughts have created your life. You are where you are because of the thoughts and decisions, actions and reactions, experiences (good and bad), and beliefs (regardless of their truth) that you have had in the past. If you don't like where you are in life, changing your thoughts will put you in a new place.

Now that, in my opinion, is useful information. If you are happy where you are, you created it. If you are not happy where you are, you created that too. Once again, the Universe is neutral in the application of the law. Whether you are creating something you want, or something you don't want, the power is in knowing you are the creator. You can create more of what you want, and less of what you don't want.

There is no limit to the creative power available to you when you understand the Law of Manifestation. With awareness and understanding, you can manifest any reality you desire. Do you want to wake up in an island paradise every morning? Put enough thoughts together to create the actions to find the island, rent the house and discover how to support yourself and you have created your paradise. Would you prefer to work for yourself instead of someone else? Create your ideal work environment utilizing your thoughts and actions around your talents, skills and abilities.

Keep in mind that beliefs are changed when you realize what is no longer working for you. Beliefs are just a collection of thoughts that you acted upon enough times that you think they are true.

For example, you work 80 hours a week and suffer from high blood pressure and IBS. The doctor suggested you make some changes in your lifestyle. You begin meditating and discover that you've been operating under the belief that there is never enough money in the bank. You realize that this belief was reinforced in childhood with statements about putting your nose to the grindstone and what happens with idle hands. Through awareness and acceptance, you shift your thought process about work and money. You start enjoying the world around you, work less, and start enjoying your new clean bill of health.

In another example, you work 80 hours a week but you meditate, exercise regularly, and eat well. You are building your dream business and you are excited to wake up every day.

The difference is in what works for you, and what doesn't. In one scenario, you are working 80 hours due to a fear of not having enough. You are creating illness in the process. In the other situation, you are creating a dream work experience and the energy is positive and uplifting.

● ● ●

PUTTING THE LAW OF MANIFESTATION INTO PRACTICE

* Manifesting happens in the present tense. Words like "I hope," "I wish," and "I want" are future tense and hold little power in the creative process. Practice replacing those phrases with "I am" and "I have" which are present tense. It may feel strange to state your intentions like they already exist but with a little practice you will become quite the expert.

* To manifest what you want in your life, spend 15 minutes a day filling in the details of your desire. Instead of saying, "I want a 3-bedroom house," consider saying "I have a 3-bedroom, 2-bath split level on a quarter of an acre in a family-friendly neighborhood." Continue adding details about the color of the house, the paint colors inside, the flooring, and whatever else tickles your fancy. The more you can picture it, the better the Universe can provide it.

* Practice engaging as many senses as possible when creating your dream. If you want to be on the beach, can you smell the ocean, feel the sun, and even taste the salty air. If your dream is a car, can you

smell the leather, hear the engine rev, and see the sun glinting off the perfect color of paint? Get excited about the details, and know that the positive energy is creating your next adventure.

* 3-D Visualization takes the practice of manifestation to the extreme. Let's use the example of a car. Imagine that you have a 3-D pen in your hand, and you can push a button and draw the car into existence. Know that everything you draw is done perfectly in proportion with no wiggly lines or weird shapes for the wheels. Once you have finished mentally drawing your desired object, release it into the Universe to the higher powers for them to handle the details.

* As you talk about what you want to create, avoid focusing on how it is going to happen, and instead focus on what you want to manifest and when you want it to happen. Quite often your brain gets bogged down in the negative vibration of how it is going to happen and that keeps the positive vibration from releasing into the field of possibility.

CHAPTER 7

The Law of Free Will

● ● ●

Every being in the Universe follows the mandates of Free Will, and cannot interfere or intervene in an action without expressed human consent.

EACH OF US INCARNATE WITH a detailed life plan that is designed to help us heal certain issues. Free Will is part of this plan. The Universal Law of Free Will states that regardless of what is predetermined, you always have the free will to alter the impact of any event or to transcend it completely. This is usually dependent on how you have lived your life up to that point. If you have been positive, loving, compassionate and demonstrated that you have healed the issue, the experience can be minimized. If you have been negative, frustrated, angry and resistant, you are demonstrating that you haven't healed the issue, and could benefit from additional experiences.

For example, I spent more than 20 lifetimes, including one in Ancient Rome, taking on an ego issue of refusing to listen to others' advice at the expense of someone's life, usually mine. I relived the same experiences over and over with only a little forward motion each lifetime. Because I continued to be negative, resistant and angry in each of those lives I continued to incarnate trying to resolve the issue.

In this lifetime, I have worked diligently to clear this karma and the resulting health issue surrounding it. I have been positive, loving and compassionate in healing the many layers. My hard work has paid off, and my guides recently showed me that there has been significant physical healing, and a cancelling of the karmic debt.

● ● ●

A Message from My Guides about Free Will

The Law of Free Will is available to all sentient beings on the planet who have displayed the conscious awareness of the other Universal laws. It is an adult law. We will use the phrase "adult law" to mean that a certain amount of growth must happen for there to be a clear understanding of this law.

When you are born, there is a natural resistance to following rules and boundaries. For example, it is a learning process to understand how to "use your words, not your hands." You learn how to use manners, follow the rules of the road, and behave appropriately in different social settings.

It is the same with learning the Universal Laws. It is necessary to understand the Universal Law of Oneness and the Universal Law of Vibration before you learn the Law of Free Will. Realizing your creative power and abilities to manifest are necessary before you can express your free will.

According to the Law of Free Will, you are a conscious being who takes complete responsibility for your fate. You understand the complexities of the other Laws, how they are interwoven, and how they affect your life and the lives of others.

As a child, you threw temper tantrums and demanded control over your life. You said, "I'll go to bed when I want!" and then you forced yourself to stay awake to make your point. You ended up falling asleep sitting up, and the adults in the room smiled at your stubbornness and persistence.

It is the same with Free Will. "I will make my own decisions. I decide where I work and who I will marry." The adults smile and allow you to exert your free will, understanding that you have just chosen the very things you planned to choose before you incarnated. (See the Law of Reincarnation, Karma, and Magnetic Affinities)

When the time is right, you do have complete Free Will and can demand it from all beings in the Universe. When that time comes, you will understand the consequences of your request on a cosmic level. You will be aware of the karmic implications and will be fully prepared.

Free Will is essential to learn as you become more fully present in your place in the Universe. Free Will allows you to be 100% responsible and aware. Most of you are still working on being completely responsible and consciously aware.

● ● ●

Putting the Law of Free Will into Practice

* If you find yourself becoming immersed in something or someone that doesn't feel good, take a few deep breaths to see how you can break free from the feeling or behavior. Ask for help from the Universe to "see what there is to see, hear what there is to hear, and know what there is to know." Remember that we only have to ask for help and help will be provided. Listen for the answers.

* As you feel more comfortable asking for help from the Universe, you may find yourself engaging higher levels of irritations - people and situations that are "yanking your chains" or engaging you in something that doesn't serve you. In these situations, practice invoking your Free Will. You can state something like: "With my Divine Free Will, I invoke the Light that serves all beings to transmute and release all negative energy and thoughts related to [fill in the blank] and I lovingly return it to the Universe."

CHAPTER 8

The Law of Attraction

● ● ●

Everything starts with the energy of a thought, and the secret to the Law of Attraction is that from there you create what you need. You have a strange idea that this life is about you getting what you want. Want is ego-based. You are here for what you need. That's the real secret.

THE LAW OF ATTRACTION IS the most well-known of the Universal Laws. Long before the book *The Secret* made its debut in 2006, Esther and Jerry Hicks were talking about the Law of Attraction through the collective consciousness called Abraham. In my opinion, Esther Hicks and Abraham are the foremost authority on Attraction. Here, I am just adding some additional insight to their wealth of information.

The briefest definition of the Law of Attraction is "like attracts like." That is, things vibrating at a certain level will attract things vibrating at a similar level. You attract things into your life that are a similar vibration as you.

References to this type of attraction exist all over the place in our society. "You become what you think about." "You reap what you sow." Or my personal favorite, "You are who you hang out with."

"You reap what you sow" makes sense. If you plant cucumber seeds, you are growing a cucumber plant, and only cucumbers can be harvested. You made a conscious decision to sow cucumber seeds.

But what if those seeds were mixed up with green been seeds and you didn't notice the difference when you planted them? When the plant started to pop out of the soil, you might be confused when its leaves are different in shape, size and color. It might take a few weeks of growth before you can notice the difference and differentiate the plants. During that time, you question what happened and wonder what went wrong.

In this example, it's easy enough to deduce what went wrong. You mixed up the seeds.

Sometimes the Law of Attraction can feel like you are planting a bucket of mixed seeds in your garden. What have you consciously planted and what was unconsciously there when you set the intention for your life? What weeds or seeds were already in the dirt at the time you dropped the seed you wanted to grow? What effect will water, sun, and fertilizer have on your plant?

The questions continue spiraling around in your head until you arrive at the one that sounds something like, "What am I doing wrong?" The answer is always that you are doing nothing wrong. You are doing everything right. You are doing everything according to plan.

That plan, the Master Plan, is what you designed prior to incarnation for the experiences you are having right now. And the experiences you had six months ago, and the ones you will have three years from now. The Master Plan is about your spiritual growth and awareness, not necessarily about driving the fastest car on the planet, or living in the biggest house in the city.

When you accept that everything happens exactly as it was designed (the Law of Magnetic Affinities), and in the exact timing that was planned (the Law of Divine Timing), you begin to get in the groove of the Law of Attraction.

You are a magnet constantly attracting situations and experiences that reflect what you are thinking and feeling. You can view these thoughts and feelings as an indication of where to focus your attention.

For example, you have just been informed that you have heart palpitations or a heart murmur. Perhaps you have had a cardiac event. You have attracted heart issues as a sign that you have work to do around love. Are you struggling with feeling loved, being loved, or connecting with others on a heart level?

In another example, you are overwhelmed by a financial burden. The bills are coming in faster than you can make the money. What thought process do you need to shift so that you resolve your money frustrations? Perhaps you believe you don't deserve to have enough money, or that having enough means others will have to do without. What is keeping you in that financial situation that doesn't feel good?

It is important to understand that you're attracting the health issues you're having in your life.

Pain anywhere in the body can generate the question, "Who or what is causing me pain?" Eye issues are about what you do not want to see. Ear problems are about who or what you do not want to hear. Hip issues are related to moving forward and accepting the emotional aspects of your life.

Dis-eases have the same energy, only more of it. First it shows up as pain, and if you work through it, it disappears. If you resist it (the Law of Resistance) or ignore it, the pain turns into disease or an illness.

Diabetes is a refusal to accept the sweetness of life. Digestive issues are difficulties swallowing, digesting or letting go of the news depending upon where the problem lies. Alzheimer's Disease is a refusal to deal with the world as it is, or a sense of hopelessness or helplessness. Anxiety disorders are about not trusting the flow and the process of life. Cancer is a deep hurt or resentment that has not been resolved.

Louise Hay has cataloged a long list of diseases and disorders and their emotional components in her book *You Can Heal Your Life*. It is a great place to start releasing the energy of a condition you have.

● ● ●

WHEN YOU WERE BORN, YOU FORGOT WHAT YOU PLANNED – A MESSAGE FROM THE AKASHIC RECORDS

When you were born, you knew you were a powerful, Divinely-connected being. You laughed and giggled, talked with angels and God, and you understood the secrets of the Universe. You knew the Universal Laws.

At some point, you started to speak the language of your family. You went through the stage of pointing at everything and demanding a name. "Dis?" "Cup." "Dis?" "Dog." And so it went on with you asking what "Dis" was, and someone giving you an answer. You were learning the language, and you were coming into agreement about what everything was called.

As you grew, you learned more of the agreements of the collective consciousness of the planet. You learned the behaviors of your culture around relationships, work, spirituality, and health. You watched with wonder at how other cultures performed the same tasks. Some you agreed with and some you did not. Those that made sense to you — the ones that you vibrated with — you kept. The behaviors and beliefs that were not a vibrational match to you were tossed out. You continue to do this checking and rechecking of vibrations but only when necessary.

Now, when you go to bed at night, you expect everything to be the same the next morning as it is every day. You have no doubt of your route to work or school, what clothes are in your closet, who your friends are, or what you will be doing on Saturday night. You have laid out your life and created it to be predictable.

Yes, there have been times when you went to bed with your world in perfect order, and you woke up with it in disarray. A family member died, a dear friend became sick, or a world event happened. You were shocked and pained, and then you adjusted. You found a way to create a new sense of normal.

Once you understand that you have created your life, you can begin to understand that if you created it, you can change it. You are not bound to the life you are living if it is not resonating with you.

You can wake up tomorrow morning and create an entirely new life, or perhaps just a part of it, depending on what works for you. From something as easily changed as the shoes you always wear to work, or as seemingly complex as changing the house you live in.

You are the creator of your life. You manifest it every day, mostly without any thought about how you want it to look. Ninety-nine point ninety-nine percent of us do not wake up thinking we can change the weather, but we can. We just don't consider it a possibility. Most of us do not wake up thinking we can change anything in our world of significance but it is always in our power to do so.

The question is: What do you want to do? What are you willing to put the time and the energy into to make something different happen? What are you willing to *think differently about? The Universal Laws say it must happen when the energy is put into the process. What do you want to make happen?*

● ● ●

THE SEVEN ASPECTS OF THE LAW OF ATTRACTION

1. Are You Aware?
   As a creature of habit, it is easy to fall into a routine and cease paying attention to the present. When you put your mind on autopilot, your drive to work becomes unnoticeable and your workday passes without much attention to what is happening. You get to the end of the day wondering what you accomplished.

   Awareness—connecting with the here and now—is the key to understanding your life. Staying conscious to the idea that everything happens exactly as it was designed, and in the exact timing that was planned, is the first step to attracting a full and abundant life.

2. Can You Accept Everything?
   Accept everything. Everything? Yes, accept everything that comes into your awareness as an experience worth having and you will find you are manifesting things out of thin air.

   But it takes practice.

   We do not always want what we are being given. The extra money in your mailbox is easy to deposit, but paying for the dent caused when you hit your neighbor's car is more difficult. It is a normal reaction to resist the negative but we know that what we resist persists. Can you find a way to accept the experiences of both good and bad?

3. Can You Allow It?
   Are you willing to plant the seed of intention and allow the thought the time and space needed to grow? Often it is difficult

to sit and wait, to be patient enough to allow the process to manifest. Your desire for instant manifestation is steeped in fear — fear of being powerless, unworthy or whatever comes up for you. Impatience and anxiety are the signals that you are not in manifesting mode.

Allowing is about trusting Divine Timing and being willing to let things unfold as they need to for your highest good. When you resist or try to manipulate the situation, you are telling the Universe that you do not trust Divine Timing.

A note about allowing. The Law of Attraction cannot be manipulated to serve your wants and desires. You can't hang pictures on the fridge or mirror of the super awesome house or car you want and recite to yourself, "I drive to work in this super awesome car" and expect it to appear.

That accounts for the conscious thoughts of what you want, but does not consider the unconscious thinking that is keeping you from achieving your desires. It's the unconscious thinking that keeps you disconnected from your creative power and Source.

Put the pictures on the fridge. Spend time with positive affirmations and then work on the thoughts, feelings, and emotions that come up around reciting them. The real work is in the suppressed thought that says, "I can't have that. I'm not worthy of that." Where did that thought come from? What story did that generate from? How can you resolve that outstanding thought? Once you've done that hard work, the car or house is easy to manifest.

4. Can You Appreciate It?
    Appreciation starts with being grateful, and ends with being amazed at what life has to offer you. It is expansive and includes the people and the things that come into your life in ways that you can't explain or completely understand. It is inclusive of every experience both good and bad.

    Appreciation is embracing all that the Universe offers on a deeply spiritual and connected level. It begins with "Thank you," and ends with "That was amazing."

5. What Do You Need to Adjust?

Your emotions are an indicator of your thoughts, and they reveal where you are directing your energy. When you do not feel good—whether physically, mentally or energetically—you are being directed to adjust your perspective and your thinking. Whether you choose to dance, sing or watch something that makes you laugh, you are consciously adjusting your energy.

Noticing when you need to adjust your attitude is critical to manifesting with the Law of Attraction. These adjustments remind me of sailing. As the captain of a sailboat, you are dependent on the direction of the wind and constantly tacking left and right to be sure you arrive at your destination. Without these adjustments, you could be off by a dozen miles.

The same is true of your emotions and attitude. Consistent adjustments to feel good allow you to arrive exactly where you intended.

6. How Do You Apply It?

Applying yourself to the process is a necessary part of walking the path. You must be actively engaged and interested in putting the Universal Laws to work. Effort and dedication are a must.

The Universe wants you to be clear about what you want. Wishing or hoping for a new car is not enough. Wanting a new car today but changing your mind about it tomorrow and changing it back the following day won't work either.

Picture the Universe as a fairy godmother ready to wave her wand to give you what you want. She's just about to cast the spell, and you change your mind. A short time later you change it back. After a few episodes of you being unclear about what you want or whether you want it, your fairy godmother sits down and waits for you to decide what you are willing to work towards.

7. Do You Really Want to Achieve It?

    You have to be willing to reach the goal and ready to achieve what you are creating. Of course it makes perfect sense but how many times have you wished for something, and then discovered you were afraid of receiving it?

    Doubt and lack of belief are very real reasons why you do not attract what you think you want. Fear of failure and fear of success are both scary and neither will help you achieve what you want.

    Sometimes your desire to attract something is bigger than your desire to achieve it. This thrill of the chase shows up everywhere, particularly in the dating scene.

    You have to be willing to attain, to own, and to achieve the goal you want without reservation. Otherwise, the Universe is going to wait until you are sure you want it.

●　　●　　●

PUTTING THE LAW OF ATTRACTION INTO PRACTICE

Here are some suggestions to help you practice attracting what you want:

*   Pick something that you would like to have. Let's use the example of a looking for a job that is more aligned with who you are. Describe what you are looking for in this new job. What exactly is your job description? Who do you work for and with? How much money do you make a year, a month, or a paycheck? Where is the job located? Keep your answers and your thoughts positive.
*   When you find yourself thinking negatively about a situation, take the time to sort through your thoughts. What happened from a neutral point of view? What were you thinking about that created the situation? What can you learn from the event?

* Be willing to do the work involved in getting what you want. You can dream about your ideal job, but if you never send out a resume, it will be difficult for the Universe to help you land it.
* Practice reciting positive affirmations about who you are, what you want, what you are becoming, and what you are creating. According to research, your brain will respond to these affirmations after 21 days of reciting them.
* Walk yourself through the seven steps of attraction listed above. Which steps trips you up? Which steps are you most comfortable with?

CHAPTER 9

The Law of Resistance

● ● ●

Consider resistance as your personality's response to what comes next.

WE LIVE IN A WORLD with resistance. Some of it is called gravity and you learn about it from a very young age. How many times have you picked up the same toy for a baby who is entertained by dropping it over and over again? Perhaps they aren't really testing the theory of gravity, but it certainly looks like it.

In high school physics, we learn about resistance when we study Ohm's Law and electrical currents. We calculate the drag or resistance on a falling object. But no one taught the Law of Resistance.

The Law of Resistance states that what you resist continues to appear in your experience until you learn to release what created the resistance in the first place. Carl Jung said it succinctly when he said, "What you resist, persists."

Every time you give energy to a thought, you are calling that into your experience. When you put positive thoughts together, you create a happy experience and you welcome it into your awareness. When you put negative, or undesirable thoughts together, you create an unhappy experience and a natural response is to push it away, ignore it, or bury it. This pushing away, or refusing to acknowledge it, creates resistance.

Resistance may look like anger, a reaction to authority, or a manipulation of the facts or people. Do you know someone who thinks others are to blame for what happens to him, the world owes him, or that he has the worst luck of anyone he knows? Perhaps he is busy being a victim and resisting taking personal responsibility for what he has created.

Resistance can appear as shame, jealousy or exhaustion. A woman who is experiencing resistance denies what has happened to her, behaves like she owns everything or everyone, or buries her head in the sand around an issue. She is busy ignoring the situation, or pushing through like a bull in a china shop.

Resistance can show up as a fear of failure or a fear of taking risks. You feel defensive, guilty, worried or anxious. Any time you feel some level of fear, you can be sure there is resistance present.

So, what does the Law of Resistance look like in real life? Let's say you want to manifest more money in your life. You ask the Universe, and it responds with you finding a $20 bill in the pocket of your jeans. Ask again, and a friend pays you the money you loaned them. Ask a third time, and you are offered a higher paying job than you have now. The first two requests for money were met with no resistance, and you were happy with the results. With the third request, you discovered that change would be involved. The new job is in another city, is a longer commute, or requires you to expand your skill set.

If you accept the new job and all the changes that it creates, you are in vibrational harmony and you feel great. If you reject the new job out of fear, worry or concern for all the changes that it may create you can count on the Law of Resistance sending you another opportunity to get comfortable with change. It might not be the exact same scenario but if your purpose is to learn to go with the flow of life, you will see a similar situation again.

Keep in mind that a repeating thought, phrase or action, done with enough repetition, accesses your unconscious mind and it will be called into your experience. Repeatedly telling stories of your extreme fear of spiders is sure to call at least one spider into your life. Repeatedly telling yourself that spiders are good for the environment and serve a useful purpose in your world is calling in a different experience.

Your conscious mind can tell the difference between a negative statement and a positive one, but your unconscious mind is fully engaged and cannot differentiate them. "I will not get sick" is a negative instruction — notice the "not." The unconscious translates that into "I will get sick" and finds ways to carry that out.

Words that energize the Law of Resistance include *don't, can't, won't* and *not*. Thinking "I can't save money" resists you being able to save money. "I won't find a job in the field I want" keeps you from finding your ideal job. "I don't know how I'm going to figure this out" keeps you from discovering an answer to your problem.

Positive statements like "I save money with every paycheck," or "The best job for me is waiting for me to apply," or "The answer to this problem will show up today" will engage the Universe to work for you. As always, you are receiving exactly what you ask for.

Whenever I find myself repeating the same unwanted pattern, I take the time to look a little deeper into the issue. In the past, I dodged telling people that I read the Akashic Records. I wasn't comfortable explaining what it was, how it works, and I wondered if they thought I was weird. Of course, I had many days, often in a row, when two or three people would ask me what I did. Each time I stressed out, stammered out an answer, and swore I was going to come up with a better answer.

Over time, I became more comfortable with the question. I practiced the answer and invited more opportunities to explain what I do. The more I prepared, the less I was asked. As I allowed myself to be uncomfortable and relax into an answer, the more the issue faded into the background.

• • •

Putting the Law of Resistance into Practice

* Notice your mood. Any time you catch yourself feeling less than good, or drifting into a negative thought, look around and see if there is something you are resisting. Noticing when something is starting to come into your awareness is always better than trying

to get rid of it after it has been there awhile. It doesn't matter what word you use to describe your bad mood. Simply being in one is a sign of resistance.

* Practice shifting your negative thought into a positive one. Transforming resistance into an empowering belief will shift you into a higher vibration.

* Raise your vibration as part of your regular routine. Listen to some upbeat music, or watch a positive television show. Go for a walk, pet your dog, or buy yourself flowers. Remember to treat yourself well to lessen the resistance in your life. Write down an action, thought or word that you would like to eliminate from your life. Take some time to consider what might be a trigger for your resistance. Can you release the trigger?

CHAPTER 10

The Law of Abundance

● ● ●

You are born with an infinite supply of everything you need to create your paradise. It is your Divine birthright.

JUST AS DOROTHY ALWAYS HAD everything she needed to get back to Kansas from the Land of Oz, you have everything you need to live in paradise. You only have to learn to look inside.

Scarcity, or the belief that there isn't enough, is the biggest lie on the planet. It was created to keep people at war with each other, arguing over resources, land, money, and more. If people are fearful of being without, then they aren't thinking about being connected to Source, their family, their neighbors or the world. Always remember that fear is the opposite of love, and love is what we are here to learn.

The truth is that you live in a Universe full of abundance and there is no lack or limitation. If you believe that there is not enough of something, your life will reflect your belief, and you will attract more of it. Notice the Law of Attraction at work.

The Law of Abundance is best represented by the sun. It shines equally on everyone in all directions. It illuminates everything, brings clarity, and helps all things to grow in a positive direction. You do not have to earn the sunshine you receive, and you do not have to worry that if the sun shines too much on your neighbor, there won't be enough left for you. There is always enough.

The reality is that the Universe has no limits, and it is constantly expanding. Following the Law of Manifestation, everything in the Universe is constantly creating and growing.

Consider for a moment how far the world has come in the last 100 years in terms of technology. Every day there is a new gadget that you did not know you needed yesterday. The Law of Abundance insures that everything that is dreamed up is created in the world. If it can be thought of, it can be created, and there is no limit to the number of thoughts you can have!

The real question regarding the Law of Abundance is why everyone is not experiencing abundance and prosperity all the time. There are three reasons.

The first is where you focus your attention. Which story do you believe? Do you believe there is an infinite supply of everything you can possibly desire? Or do you believe you have to conserve your energy, save your money, and that there is never enough? Notice that there is no right answer. Whichever you believe is right for you.

The second reason everyone isn't experiencing abundance all the time is that you get what you believe you deserve. Are you worthy enough for abundance? Do you believe that you deserve everything that life has to offer? What is keeping you from believing anything different?

The third reason is that you have not learned how to receive infinite abundance. Ironically, you know innately how to receive it, but more than likely the world has conditioned it out of you. How many times have you heard, "Money does not grow on trees" or "You do not always get what you want?" What other conditioned responses have you heard?

● ● ●

Putting the Law of Abundance into Practice

❄ Ask yourself how are you already living a life of abundance? Make a list of the people who are in your life, the things you own, experiences you've had and the places you've been. Consider the intangible things as well, such as love and happiness. Does everyone have these things and experiences?

❦ Release the need to control the situations in your life. Most often when you begin to feel that there isn't enough, the natural instinct is to grab, seize, and take control. This comes from the false idea that you have to push and shove to get what you want. The opposite is true. Take the blooming of a flower or a bouquet, for example. Allow the flowers to bloom instead of prying the flowers open.

❦ Practice receiving the blessings and abundance that come to you on a regular basis. Be grateful for what you have and thank the Universe for what comes to you. It is easy to take waking up for granted until the ability is no longer there. The more you appreciate what is there, the more the Universe will provide you with what you ask for.

CHAPTER 11

The Law of Reflection

● ● ●

Everyone needs a mirror to see what is not normally accessible to you. This includes the black smudge on your nose as well as the one on your heart.

THE LAW OF REFLECTION IS a mirror that the Universe uses to reveal your inner thoughts, opinions, and perspectives. Without fail, it reflects your most sacred values, firmly held beliefs, and personal bias. You can count on every situation and every single person in your life to reflect your inner thinking.

There's no judgment involved in this reflection. Your thoughts don't make you bad; your opinions don't make you better off. The Law is only asking you to listen, notice what you say and think about others as a mirror of yourself. It is asking you to notice how you act and react to situations in your life, and if you can see them as a reflection of your feelings and opinions. It is your job to notice what is there and decide what to do about it.

There are two types of reflections.

The first reflects characteristics that you admire. What you admire in others is something you recognize in yourself. These are easy to understand and accept.

"Betty is so well organized and runs the book club like a well-oiled machine" is a statement which shows that you like order, organization and people who can be counted on. "Bob really knows how to treat women. He's so thoughtful to his wife and daughters" shows how much you value thoughtfulness.

The second reflects characteristics that you dislike and want to avoid. These characteristics can be difficult or downright impossible to accept. They are characteristics you may recognize in yourself. You may be aware of them or you might have pushed them into your subconscious. Perhaps your friends and family are aware of them, and have even brought them to your attention.

"Mary is so bossy and thinks she owns the place" is an opportunity for you to look at your ideas about ordering people around. Do you value it, or does it tick you off? Is it connected to a story in childhood, maybe an older sibling who always told you what to do? Perhaps you want to look at your ideas about being bossed around. What are you holding on to, or resisting letting go?

"Fred can't make a decision to save his life" is a chance to look at your ideas about indecisiveness. "Did you see how old Chrissy looks?" is asking you to question your thoughts about aging.

Keep in mind if the Universe really wants to draw your attention to something, it will continually repeat the same message in different ways. You may continue to meet the same type of people, or to attract similar situations. Look at some of these unconventional ways that it can get the message to you to re-examine your beliefs and ways of thinking.

Water reflects what is happening to your emotions. Perhaps your faucet is leaking, or a pipe bursts in your house. Ask yourself how your emotions are leaking, or where you have unshed tears or unresolved emotional issues.

A fire in the fireplace or a campfire may indicate a peaceful, comfortable situation while an out of control wildfire reflects the anger and hostility of all those affected by it. Fire clears and transmutes negative energy. When a house burns to the ground, perhaps there is a deeper reason than a pan left on the stove.

Air is energy, and it spiritually represents communication and new ideas. A hurricane or strong winds blow away outmoded thinking and brings in new ways of doing things. A breezy day clears away the dust and dirt and creates needed shifts.

When you are aware of the Universal Law of Reflection, you'll understand that everything that happens in your life is a message from the

Universe. If your car's brakes need replacing, you can ask yourself where you need to slow down but you haven't? If your car is dented in the parking lot of the grocery store, ask yourself how are you feeling beat up?

Even your pet's diagnosis is a message for you. Pets take on our excess issues and pain as part of their agreement with us, so this would be a good time to ask yourself what is the meaning of your pet's illness.

Whatever comes into your life, look into the proverbial mirror and see what it has to teach you. Once you understand the Law of Reflection, you can expand your spiritual growth by looking at what life is showing you.

● ● ●

Putting the Universal Law of Reflection into Practice

* When something out of the ordinary occurs in your life, take the time to ask yourself what the message might be. Remember that messages can be positive or negative to you, but that the Universe is neutral. Whether a pipe in your house breaks, or you get an unexpected break at work, see how the Universe is providing for you.

* Be willing to look at yourself in a neutral light to see what others might see in you. Think about two people that you admire, and what you admire about them. How does that quality show up in you? Is it something you already have and like, or are you cultivating it? Think about two people who you do not relate to, and what bothers you about them. How does that characteristic show up in you? Is it something you dislike, or is there a story around that quality for you?

* When a tragedy is brought to your attention, use it as an opportunity to examine your own life. A tragic flood inspires you to look at what needs to be washed away, or a sudden death brings an awareness of who to express love towards.

CHAPTER 12

The Law of Correspondence

● ● ●

The Universe cannot contradict itself or its laws in any way. There are no exceptions. Each law has a specific purpose and cannot be altered.

IT IS REASSURING TO KNOW that there is only one set of rules that the Universe plays by: The Universal Laws.

That hasn't always been the case on our planet. By agreement, earth has been the one place in the Universe where a different set of rules have been in play.

For example, there are many different rules for imprisonment in the world. Depending on your status in society, politics, career and who you know, you may serve time in prison for the same crime as another person with a different set of circumstances. The homeless, poor and disenfranchised serve longer and tougher sentences than the rich and well-connected for the same crime.

This is not the case in the Universe. There are no contradictions or different rules for different beings. Exceptions do not exist, and there are no alterations, touch-backs, frontsies, or special clauses.

With the ushering in of the Aquarian Age [the astrological age that changes roughly every 2,150 years that relates to the sun's position at the spring equinox], the Law of Correspondence is in full effect, and the Universe is cleaning house. Old regimes, political families, ruling classes, and the outdated paradigms are being dissolved and cleared. Deep programming is being exposed for examination and transmuting. We are constantly being asked to look at what we think we know, and what we think we believe.

The phrase "as above, so below" refers to the Law of Correspondence. It translates to what happens in heaven, happens on earth. The rules that apply to the rest of the Universe apply to us as well. The phrase "as within, so without" also refers to the Law of Correspondence, and translates to what you see within you, you can also see around you. This helps you clean out what no longer works in your life.

The man who thoughtlessly leaves his trash on the table next to you at lunch irritates you. You angrily stand up, collect his trash and throw it in the nearby garbage. Why are you so aggravated? With a little thought, you remember how your mom made you pick up all the trash in the house but never made your brother pick up the trash or do housework. Boys did not need to know how to do housework in your mother's world.

The question is whether that irritation was more about the man who didn't pick up his trash or more about the feeling of not being treated fairly as a child? The Law of Correspondence says it is more about being treated unfairly, and it asks you to look deeper at the emotion behind your irritation and clear that out.

It is important to remember that your underlying belief attracts the situations and people into your life for you to look at the belief and release it. Why do you hold that belief about being treated unfairly? What other times have you felt that way? How can you sweep that out of your thinking?

If you believe that you have to serve others, you will attract people who need to be looked after in some way. Why are you in service to others, or why do you need to be needed?

If you believe that no one understands you, you will find people drawn to you that do not understand you. Why do you believe that you cannot be understood?

If you believe that you are unworthy, you will find yourself in one relationship after another with people who do not value your worth. Why don't you value yourself more?

The reverse is also true.

If you see yourself as a positive addition to a team, you will attract members who value your opinion and your work. If you are a supportive friend willing to be inconvenienced to help someone out, you will find that many people are available to help you.

Your inner emotions, thoughts, and feelings attract the outer actions, words and responses. If there is something in your outer world that does not work for you, look inside and recognize the thought or pattern and shift how you are thinking. You will instantly attract different people and experiences.

● ● ●

Putting the Law of Correspondence into Practice

- When you find yourself having a bad day or a negative experience, take the time to ask yourself what the Universe is trying to tell you.
- Imagine yourself floating down a lazy river with nothing but time on your hands. As you completely let go and let your mind wander, realize that this moment is perfect exactly as it is. What is it about this experience that is working for you? If you find yourself moving into thinking about when this time will be over, consider what takes you out of the present and into worrying about the future. What takes you out of the present and feeling guilty about the past?
- Take the time to consider what is not working in your life, and ask yourself what is happening inside that may be creating the outside event. If your relationship isn't working, ask what your beliefs are and why you think the way you do. It might involve some deep work to get to the truth but it's worth the time. Your outer world will shift as you release what is tripping you up in your thoughts.
- Do the difficult task of taking full responsibility for what is happening in your life, both the good and the bad. Sometimes it's easier to take responsibility for one and not the other. Do you take credit for the good but hide from the bad? Do you step up to take the responsibility for the bad, but struggle to think of the good things that are happening?

CHAPTER 13

The Law of Compensation

● ● ●

You are always compensated for every thought, word, action or deed. Notice that it is every thought, word, action or deed, not just the good ones. Remember good and bad are human constructs. Universal consciousness is neutral. Everything is compensated. Always.

WHEN MY CHILDREN WERE YOUNG my husband taught them his "boomerang theory." Just like the boomerang, what you throw out is what comes back to you. Say kind words and kind words will be said about you. Be generous with what you have and others will share in return. It was a useful analogy for our kids because it was so clear to understand, and they saw it in effect time and time again.

Sometimes they saw it from the positive perspective: "Mom, I shared my lunch with Rachel, and she gave me some of her dessert." Sometimes they saw it from the negative perspective: "I hit John with the ball and he hit me back." They learned that the Universe is neutral in its response.

It doesn't change when we become adults. The Universal Law of Compensation states that what you put out into the world comes back to you in at least equal measure. Smile at everyone you pass on the street, and you will feel amazing by the time you reach the end of the block. Talk trash about a coworker and you will stumble upon a similar conversation that two coworkers are having about you.

Another aspect of this Law is that you can never be compensated for more than what you have put in. For example, your income today is compensation for the work you did in the past. If you want to make more money, you have to put more value into your work. The same is true about your mental attitude and feelings. Your thinking today reflects what you have been feeding yourself in terms of hopes, dreams, and creative ideas. If you want to be more positive tomorrow than you are today, you'll have to put more uplifting thoughts in tonight.

The Law of Compensation can be seen everywhere. Pay your debts quickly and honestly, and see others treat you in the same way. Donate whatever you have in terms of time, money, and love without consideration of what you will get in return, and you will see the blessings come back to you in ways that you surprise you. Make it a habit to do more than what you are paid for, and discover the rewards both financially and emotionally.

Just be sure to note that the Law of Compensation is neutral in its application. Positive in means more positive out, and negative in means more negative out. If you choose to complain about a situation, you are going to see more of that negative situation. If you are stingy with your time or your money, you are going to see people everywhere who behave the same with you.

● ● ●

PUTTING THE LAW OF COMPENSATION INTO PRACTICE

* Give what you have available to give and see the Universe respond to you. Keep in mind that money is not the only way to give. If you have time to do something for your community, give that and it will be given back to you. If you have clothes, furniture or a skill, give that to those who will benefit from it.
* Watch your words and actions, and be mindful that you are putting out what you want to see returned to you. It is a challenge for even the most mindful to practice kind and thoughtful words and actions.

* Consider the amount of time you "give" to watching television and reading about local news and world events. Keep in mind that these activities are also counted in the Law of Compensation. It is easy to become overloaded with the opinions expressed in the media, but you can practice recognizing the challenges in the world while keeping them in perspective.

CHAPTER 14

Are There Other Universal Laws?

● ● ●

YES, THERE ARE OTHER UNIVERSAL Laws. While I was researching the Laws, I saw more than 100 laws! After checking with my Masters, Teachers and Loved Ones, the list was narrowed to the 13 Laws that they felt were the most important to learn and easy to apply. They emphasized that everyone starts at the beginning.

For your reference, here is a quick review of some of the additional Laws. As I mentioned in the beginning of the book, there are subtle differences in the wording and energy of the Laws.

The Law of Request states that we should always ask others for what we want with clarity and intention. We should never impose ourselves on others, or expect that others are waiting to help us.

The Law of Projection states that while everything reflects what we see, we project what we see outward for the world to see.

The Law of Attachment states that we can have anything we want in life if we are not attached to it. As soon as we are dependent on it, we can be controlled and manipulated by the very thing we wanted.

The Law of Attention states that an outcome manifests to the exact percentage of attention you give to it. Attention is the focus of your thoughts, words and action.

The Law of Flow states that nothing is static and everything is always moving. When one thing is taken away, another thing will move in to take its place.

The Law of Clarity states that what you are clear about will manifest instantly.

The Law of Intention states that intention releases a force that is more powerful than wishes, hopes and dreams. The power of intention moves ideas into manifestation.

The Law of Prosperity states that you will receive only as much as you believe. If you do not believe that you deserve being prosperous, or if you have a fear of being prosperous, you will not be.

The Law of Success happens when you come into vibrational harmony with your desires and actions. Success is guaranteed when you believe in yourself.

The Law of Polarity states that everything has an opposite. Hot has cold, and up has down.

The Law of Balance creates stability in that every thought is balanced by whoever creates it. It allows all viewpoints without feeling that you must defend your own. Love is the great balance.

The Law of Responsibility happens when you no longer blame other people or situations for what has happened in your life. True response-ability happens when you respond to the needs of everyone and everything around you with love.

The Law of Fellowship states that when two or more people of similar vibration join together for a shared purpose, the energy that is created is multiplied by two, three, or even four times.

The Law of Discrimination and Discernment occurs when you are given guidance from the Universe and you have learned to check internally to see if it feels right to you.

The Law of Challenge gives you the right to use your discernment and discrimination to challenge what might not be in alignment for your highest good.

The Law Affirmation states that you bring about what you affirm. It is the understanding that the Universe rearranges itself to give you what you believe.

The Law of Meditation states that when you still your mind long enough to quiet the chatter, you will connect to God, Source, Creator and receive the wisdom you are seeking.

The Law of Miracles allows your lower energy and denser vibration to be transmuted by the higher vibrations of God, Source, Creator. By asking for Divine assistance, you receive what some perceive as synchronicities and coincidences, and others call miracles.

The Law of Healing states that healing happens when high frequency energy transmutes the negativity of disease. The empty space is replaced with love and light.

The Law of Perspective allows you to see beyond normal human understanding. Perspective allows you to see without judgment, fear and resistance. It allows you to commune with spirits, angels and other entities of the spiritual realm.

The Law of Gratitude and Grace allows true grace and gratitude to be the key of abundance that unlocks everything in the Universe. When you are grateful for whatever you have, more is available to you.

CHAPTER 15

How to Be in Alignment

● ● ●

YOU'VE READ THE BOOK AND completed the exercises to understand the Universal Laws. Now you can integrate the Laws into your life. You can practice being in alignment with who you are on a spiritual level and what your purpose is in this lifetime.

When you are working in alignment with the plans that the Universe has for you, you are in the zone. Problems dissolve with little issue or concern, people return your e-mails, phone calls and texts, and deliveries are made on time.

When you are in alignment, you are in a higher state of consciousness and awareness. The Universe is conspiring to make things happen for you. Things become simpler and your desires appear right before your eyes. The world begins to respond to your thoughts.

Here are the 10 steps to finding that alignment:

Step 1: Understand that everything and everyone is connected. (The Law of One)

Step 2: Be clear that you have created your life for the experiences that you are having. You have the power. Your life isn't being done to you. (The Laws of Magnetic Affinities, Free Will, Reincarnation and Karma)

Step 3: Remember that you have the free will to decide how your life will turn out. Stay positive. It always works out. (The Laws of Free Will, Divine Timing, and Vibration)

Step 4: Understand that everything begins with a thought or an idea. Guard your thoughts and you will design the life of your dreams. (The Laws of Manifestation, Vibration, and Attraction)

Step 5: Remember when you are not feeling right, you can act on it. Notice that when you feel out of alignment, decisions and actions are difficult and are not flowing; you are uncomfortable, restless, and angry. (The Laws of Vibration, Attraction, Resistance, and Reflection)

Step 6: Question your feelings and the belief system that is playing out when you notice you are out of alignment. Acknowledge when you say "I can't do it," "No one else understands," "It's too much work," "It costs too much," or "It won't work." Hear those phrases or similar ones as a signal to do some inner work. (The Laws of Vibration, Attraction, Resistance, and Reflection)

Step 7: Reassure yourself that you are supporting yourself whether anyone else is there for you. You are paying attention. You love yourself no matter what has happened. (The Laws of Vibration, Correspondence, and Compensation)

Step 8: Release the control and release the fear by loving yourself. Repeat your loving statements until you no longer feel the fear and control. (The Laws of Resistance and Correspondence)

Step 9: Seek help from others. That is what your friends are here to do — to help you sort out your emotions. (The Laws of Magnetic Affinities and Reincarnation and Karma)

Step 10: Raise your vibration. If you are struggling, you are in a lower vibration. Dance it out, create, color, seek out nature, reset, or work it out at the gym. As your vibration shifts you will begin to attract more of what you want. (The Laws of Vibration, Manifestation, and Attraction)

● ● ●

As you find your alignment, you may notice more coincidences in your life. We tend to think of these chance happenings as rare events but when we are in alignment it ceases to feel like a coincidence.

These are signs from the Universe, and it's better not to brush them off. Your guides on the other side are helping you and they appreciate the love, gratitude, and recognition. You did not just happen to be in line for coffee with the president of the company that you most want to work for, with your resume in your hand, by chance. Thank your benevolent beings.

The same is true for all the following ways that the Universe is communicating with you:

Recurring Experiences

When the same type of event keeps happening repeatedly throughout the day, or at the same time every day, look around. Do you keep having the same kind of conversation with different people on the elevator? Are you seeing a similar message on billboards, road signs and magazines? Do you hear the same song on the radio no matter where you are? What is the Universe trying to get you to notice?

Dreams

Your dreams are your access to your unconscious mind and to the Universe. For most people, it is the time when you are the most available for messages. What are you dreaming about? What is the interpretation of those dreams?

Songs/Music/Lyrics

Do you find yourself with an earworm that you cannot shake? Earworms are those bits of songs that you keep singing over and over again. It is particularly interesting when you notice the words that you are singing, whether they are the actual lyrics or ones you have made up. Is there an answer to a question in what you keep repeating over and over in your head?

Animals

The natural world provides many message delivery systems to us through animals. Googling spirit animals or totems will give you access to a long list of animals, insects, reptiles and birds that have a variety of meanings. Animals are spiritual beings and are teachers, messengers and holders of ancient wisdom.

Repeatedly seeing the same animal or animal behavior can be a strong sign of an unfulfilled desire or outcome. Seeing a squirrel might mean you are in the park, but it is also a message to have more fun, lighten your load, and relieve some stress. Seems like a great time to act like a kid and go down the slide, or swing a little!

Patterns of Numbers

Do you keep glancing at your clock or watch at a certain time like 11:11 or 4:44? Does the same number pattern show up on your store receipts, or the balance in your checking account? It doesn't matter where it shows up. These repeating patterns of numbers are messages from the Universe.

Repeating ones carry the vibration of new beginnings. The Universe is supporting you to act, make a change or begin again.

Repeating twos carry the vibration of love and acceptance. The Universe is asking you to trust your heart, express deep emotions, and forgive yourself and/or others.

Repeating threes carry the vibration of creation and joy. The Universe supports you in all areas to co-create and manifest with the Divine. Express and open yourself up to the world so you can tap into your potential and explore new parts of you.

Repeating fours carry the vibration of hopes and dreams. The Universe wants you to know that you can achieve everything, and you are on the right path. Lay the groundwork and believe in yourself because financial abundance is on the way.

Repeating fives carry the vibration of change and letting go of all that does not serve you to make way for the new and positive aspects. The Universe wants you to be open to the opportunities that show up for you.

Repeating sixes carry the vibration of grace to neutralize ego and fear. The Universe wants you to refocus on the abundance and beauty around you instead of fear and lack. Trust that all your needs are being met and focus on the magic of what's around you.

Repeating sevens carry the vibration of intuition, knowing that you are on the right path and that you can follow your hunches even without evidence. The Universe wants you to trust yourself and not allow other's opinions and feelings to sway your decisions.

Repeating eights carry the vibration of growth and transformation. The Universe is alerting you that you have moved through a cycle of change and that you are coming out on the other side with new energy and joy. It is a reminder that you have done the work, and the reward is on the way.

Repeating nines carry the vibration of clarity and emptiness, a clearing out of the old to make way for the new. The Universe is asking you to empty your thoughts and mind to get clear about a new opportunity. A teacher is on the way, or a spiritual lesson is around the corner.

Recurring Words/Phrases

Just like recurring experiences, if you find yourself hearing, reading or seeing the same words or phrases, the Universe is sending you a message. Before I decided to write this book, I bumped into three different people who mentioned that if I wanted to write a book they would be happy to help me get started!

Unexpected Meetings or Chance Encounters

Is there such a thing as chance? You are standing in line to buy an ice cream at a place you never go and the person you were hoping to meet is in line behind you. Pay attention. The Universe is sending you a very clear message.

Your Gut Feelings

Always follow your gut instincts. Just like dreams, your intuition or gut reaction to something, someone or some place is trying to send you a message. It is your unconscious thoughts leading you to or away from something. Practice tuning in often.

Unusual Words or Phrases

When you hear a word or phrase that seems out of sync with the situation or time, one that you haven't heard in a very long time, or that reminds you of someone or something, pay attention. When someone overheard "Did you feel like you were tiptoeing through the tulips," my friend instantly knew that her deceased aunt agreed with her decision to go slow with her new relationship. It was a private phrase they joked about before her aunt's death.

● ● ●

The Common Block of Fear

The more you embrace being in alignment with your spiritual side and your purpose, the more you may discover a block, or a place where you are stuck. This stuckness can show up as a recurring illness, anger directed at no one in particular, a repeating of a similar situation, or a feeling of unresolved frustration. It can show up in an endless number of ways. Some of us yell and scream, others retreat. Regardless of how you express your stuckness, the common block is fear.

How does fear show up for you?

Do you have a fear of success? Do you wonder what you will do if everything works out and you are accomplishing everything you set out to do? Perhaps you fear not being able to be higher, faster or more next time. Are you concerned that people will not understand your motivation and drive to do more?

Just as there is a fear of success, there is a fear of failure. A fear of failure can keep you from reaching for your dreams. What if you put all your effort into getting what you want and it doesn't work out or that it isn't what you want? Anticipating what you will do then, or say to the people around you can leave you hesitant to decide. How will you resolve the possible ramifications?

There is also a fear of being judged, ridiculed or not liked. It does not get any easier once you are off the playground in elementary school. You want to be accepted and loved more than anything else in life, and the possibility that you will not be can keep you from moving forward.

Perhaps you have experienced the feeling of not deserving whatever the Universe has in store for you. That's the fear of not being good enough.

Maybe you were taught not to ask for anything for yourself, that to be selfish was a sin against God. Maybe you have low self-esteem, and need a boost in the "I am Powerful" department.

There is also the fear of lack, or the belief in scarcity. Lifetimes of suffering from not enough food, love, compassion—to name a few—create a real worry that there isn't enough in the world of whatever you need. Do you have a fear that there isn't enough for both you and your neighbor? When you believe in the Law of Abundance and you know you can have it all, I can have it all, and so can everyone else on the planet. No one goes without. The idea that there isn't enough is an old thought that can be tossed in the garbage.

● ● ●

PUTTING ALIGNMENT INTO PRACTICE

Besides implementing the 10 steps to being in alignment, here are some additional ways to practice the concepts in this chapter.

- Notice the coincidences that are happening around you. Are you having the same dream every night? If you are, check out a dream interpretation website to get some insight into what your subconscious might be trying to tell you. Are you hearing the same phrase repeated? What does that phrase mean to you?
- Get into the habit of noticing the thoughts, feelings and reactions of your body. Do you have a certain vibe when you walk into a new friend's house? Do you feel on alert when a particular person is around you? Spend some time giving credence to those emotions and vibes. You aren't wrong.
- If you feel yourself getting frustrated, angry, or having an unusual emotion, give yourself a timeout. Ask yourself what is disturbing you, and listen for the answer. Be willing to be surprised by what you might hear and learn. You are always getting valuable new information about yourself if you are open to the possibility.

•   •   •

ONE MORE MESSAGE

THIS JOURNEY HAS NOT BEEN just mine. My daughter, Sarah, helped me put my work with the Universal Laws into perspective as we sat talking over book edits.

"You and Dad have been teaching Matthew and me about the Universal Laws our whole lives. We learned about the Law of Attraction as putting positive energy into the world and being able to watch our perspectives shift. The Law of Divine Timing was about being exactly where you are supposed to be to learn the lesson and move forward. While you did not label them as 'The Universal Laws' back then, they have always been the voice in our heads. And here you are sharing them with the world!"

Now you, the reader, have this information too; along with some divine insight and practical ways to implement the Universal Laws into your every-day life. As my Masters, Teachers, and Loved Ones have said:

We want you to know the Universal Laws. We want you to know how powerful you are. We want you to once again remember the secrets of the Universe. It is your Divine right.

You are ready now. You've been given another nudge to achieve everything you designed for your life. Remember that you already know this. Remember that you are loved. Remember that you are part of God.

ABOUT THE AUTHOR

• • •

BONNIE SAX IS A GIFTED Akashic Records heal-
ing practitioner and teacher living in South
Florida who infuses spiritual wisdom into
everyday life. With awareness and a clear
knowing, Bonnie sees old patterns and resistance, reveals resentments and fears for the
stories that they are. She has an amazing
ability to take the most complex spiritual
wisdom and put it into easily understandable analogies.

While she thoroughly enjoys the practice of reading the Akashic Records
for herself and others, Bonnie is crystal clear that she is here to teach people
about the Universal Laws, and to guide them through the process of dissolv-
ing their old paradigms and ways of viewing the world.

Private readings with Bonnie can be scheduled through her website,
www.BonnieSax.com. She teaches online and in-person classes on the
Universal Laws and the Akashic Records. If you or somebody you know
would be interested in hosting Bonnie as a guest speaker or blogger, she
would love to work with you! You can email her at Bonnie@BonnieSax.com.

REFERENCES

• • •

Here are some additional sources of information you may enjoy:

WEBSITES

www.BonnieSax.com
Register for classes on the Universal Laws, the Akashic Records, and healing your spirit; schedule appointments for Akashic Records readings; sign-up to receive bi-weekly newsletters about upcoming events and stay up-to-date with Bonnie's promotional schedule.

www.8thChakra.com
Dedicated to guiding humanity to connect with enlightened practices that re-mind us of who we are and why we are here. Join the Enlightened Humanity Project™, hosted online by Bonnie and Lily Z. Winsaft, to participate in lively, inspirational themed discussions and to receive healing through the Akashic Records and Theta-Healing.

www.AkashicStudies.com
The official website for Dr. Linda Howe, author of *How to Read the Akashic Records*, *Healing Through the Akashic Records*, and *Discover Your Soul's Path Through the Akashic Records*. These are the books that Bonnie references in her Akashic Records class and the modality she utilizes to access the Akashic Records.

<u>www.IntegrativeNutrition.com</u>
The official website for the Institute for Integrative Nutrition, which is the largest nutrition school and certification program for health coaches in the world. Bonnie is a graduate of IIN.

<u>www.Masaru-Emoto.net</u>
Dr. Masaru Emoto is renowned for his study on the messages of love and hate displayed in frozen water crystals. His research reflects that words are the vibration of nature and in that he understood that beautiful words created beautiful nature and ugly words created ugly nature.

● ● ●

BOOKS

Ask and It Is Given: Learning to Manifest Your Desires by Esther and Jerry Hicks (The Teachings of Abraham)

Getting into the Vortex: Guided Meditations CD and User's Guide by Esther and Jerry Hicks (The Teachings of Abraham)

How to Read the Akashic Records by Linda Howe

Healing Through the Akashic Records by Linda Howe

Discover Your Soul's Path Through the Akashic Records by Linda Howe

Conversations with History: Inspiration, Reflections, and Advice from History-Makers and Celebrities on the Other Side by Susan Lander

The Little Soul and the Sun by Neale Donald Walsch

76366983R00049

Made in the USA
Columbia, SC
07 September 2017